Mah Jong

One Step at aTime

by

Alain Gelbman

Ishi Press International
San Jose • London

Published by

Ishi Press International

76 Bonaventura Drive
San Jose, CA 95134

20 Bruges Place
London NW1 0TE

Printed in U.S.A.

TABLE OF CONTENTS

INTRODUCTION

Mah Jong is an ancient Asian game of skill and luck, surprisingly similar to Rummy. There are Suits and most playing pieces (called "Tiles") are arranged in sequential order, reminescent of the familiar 52 card deck. Depending on where in the world the game is played, different rules are followed. I chose the rules promulgated by the Japan Mah Jong Association as described in Eleanor Noss Whitney's *A Mah Jong Handbook*, Charles E. Tuttle Co., 1964, and *Mah Jong for Beginners* by Shozo Kanai and Margaret Farrell, Charles E. Tuttle Co., 1955. With the exception of additional ways to score Doubles, the popular variation of the game in Japan is nearly identical to the official one described here.

The American rules pertaining to exchanging Tiles and scoring extra Doubles were not adopted in this manual. For a discussion of these rules, see: *Mah Jong, Anyone?*, by Kitty Strauser and Lucille Evans, Charles E. Tuttle, 1964; or, *Learn To Play Mah Jongg* by Marcia Hammer, David McKay Co., 1979.

I attempted to distill the rules to their simplest elements and I limited the use of esoteric terms as much as possible. This way I hope to make the game of Mah Jong more accessible and appealing. I have kept rituals to a minimum and I shortened the process to choose the First Leader. You'll spend as much time as possible playing the game.

Mah Jong game sets can be purchased in most game stores and in Oriental gift shops. To protect your set, play on a cloth covered surface.

My objective for this manual is to make Mah Jong as appealing and easy to learn as possible. Playing Mah Jong has given me many hours of pleasure in the company of friends — some of whom I met through this game. I wish the same for you and hope to contribute to your fun in this way.

Alain

Very special thanks to Erica Sanders and Janet Wright.

MAH JONG

Playing the game of Mah Jong can be broken down into the following processes:

1. Setting up the Deal and building a Winning Hand (pp.5-20),
2. Scoring the Winning Hand (pp.21-32), and
3. Paying the winner(page 33).

THE GAME SET

ACCESSORIES

 A wheel or a die displaying the 4 Winds. Used to indicate the Round Wind, **it is kept by the First Leader.**

Dice with one to six dots on each side. Used to select the First Leader and to determine the Deal. **They are kept by the Leader at the time of play.**

STICKS

Denominations:	Not used in official play	500 points	100 pts.	10 pts.

Denominations and amounts distributed to each player at the beginning of the game:

(Highest denomination not used)

500 pts.	(2 each)
100 pts.	(9 each)
10 pts.	(10 each)
Total =	2000 points

Note: If sticks did not come with your game set, simply use any other tokens in the 3 denominations shown above.

THE TILES

HONOR TILES

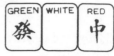

Winds
East   South   West   North

Dragons
Green   White   Red

SUIT TILES

Coins

Characters

Bamboos

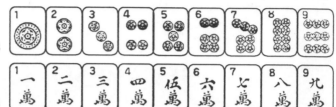

Note: The 1 of Bamboos is depicted by a bird or other symbol, and it is inscribed with the number 1 in the corner.

External Suit Tiles (1's & 9's)

Internal Suit Tiles (2's through 8's)

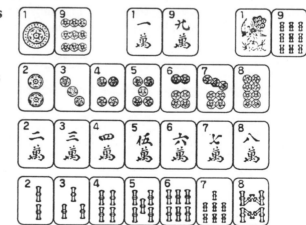

There are 4 of each Tile, for a total of 136 Tiles

In addition to the Tiles introduced above, your game set may include other Tiles depicting Flowers, Seasons, Jokers, etc... These are used in the American and possibly other versions. Since we do not need them here, you might use these extra Tiles to replace lost or broken ones.

PLAYING

OBJECT OF THE GAME

The winner will be the first player to complete a hand containing 1 Pair plus 4 Sets as shown.

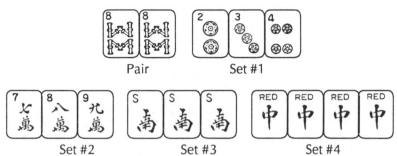

Pair   Set #1

Set #2   Set #3   Set #4

Sets #1 and #2 are "Runs" (consecutive series of 3 Tiles in the same suit)
   Only Suit Tiles can form Runs.
   Honor Tiles cannot form Runs.

Set #3 is a "Triple", and Set #4 is a "Quad".
   The Pair, Triples, and Quads can be formed
   with both Honor and Suit Tiles.

The 4 Sets may be any combination of Runs, Triples, and/orQuads.

DEFINITIONS

1. **Pair**: 2 identical
    Tiles:

2. **Set**: A Run, a Triple, or a Quad.

3. **Run**: A Set of 3 consecutive Tiles in the same Suit
    (only **3** Tiles in a Run)

 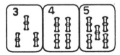 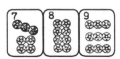

Note: Only Suit Tiles can form Runs, Honor Tiles cannot form Runs.

4. **External Run**: A Run that contains an External Tile; that is, a "**1**,2,3" or a "7,8,**9**".

5. **Triple**: A Set of 3 identical Tiles.

6. **Quad**: A Set of all 4 identical Tiles.

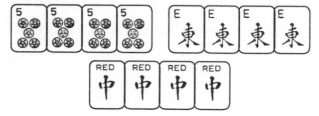

7. **The Wall**: The Tiles arranged in a square, ready to be drawn.

8. **Self Drawn Tile**: A Tile drawn directly from the Wall.

9. **Discard**: A Tile cast away as least desirable in the hand. A Discarded Tile may be claimed by another player under certain conditions listed below.

10. **Concealed Set**: All the Tiles are Self Drawn from the Wall (the Set contains no Discards). The Concealed Set is kept hidden in the hand.

11. **Melded Set**: A Set that contains 1, and only 1, Discard. The Melded Set is displayed visible to the other players.

12. **Winning Tile**: The last Tile that completes the hand for the win.

13. **Complete Hand**: The Winning Hand containing 1 Pair plus 4 Sets.

Shuffling

The tiles are assembled in the middle of the table, face down and mixed, usually with both hands, by all the players.

Building the Wall

Each player forms two lines of 17 tiles each, face down. One line is stacked on top of the other. All four players' stacked lines are arranged in a square called the Wall.

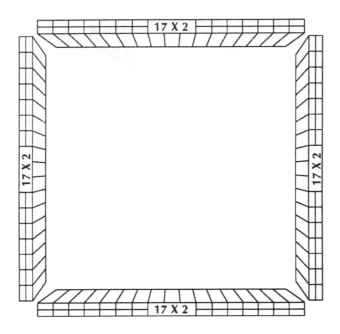

Selecting the First Leader and Assignment of Own Wind

Officially, this process is quite complex. For an easier method, each player rolls one die, the one getting the highest number is the First Leader. The Leader is always East as "Own Wind". Next to the Leader in play, on the right, sits the player whose "Own Wind" is South. Next (across from East), sits West, and to the right of West sits the player whose "Own Wind" is North (see picture on top of next page).

Seating Arrangement

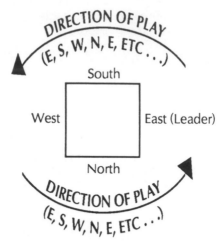

Beginning the Deal

To determine where the Deal begins, the Leader (East) throws 2 dice. The number indicated is counted off in the direction of play, beginning with East, then South, then West, then North, then East, and so on.

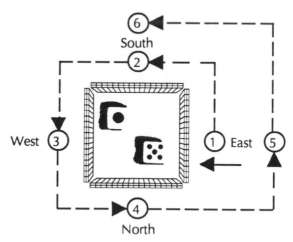

In this case, the dice show 6, which is South.

The player designated by the dice throws the dice again and the numbers of both castings are added.

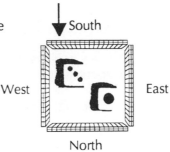

West | | East

South throws the dice again, they show 4. Both castings total 10.

North

Starting from the right end of his or her own side of the Wall, the player designated previously counts as many stacks of tiles as indicated by the <u>total of both castings</u>. The Deal begins at the very next stack.

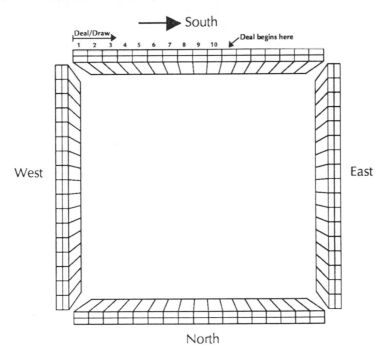

*South counts 10 stacks beginning on the **right**.*
The Deal begins with the 11th stack.

If both castings add up to more than 17, counting proceeds around the corner, and the Deal begins in front of the player on the left (in this example, in front of East).

SEQUENCE OF PLAY, AND DIRECTION FOR DRAWING TILES:

The sequence of play begins with East, then South, then West, then North, then East, etc... (or counter-clockwise).

Tiles are drawn from the Wall clockwise.

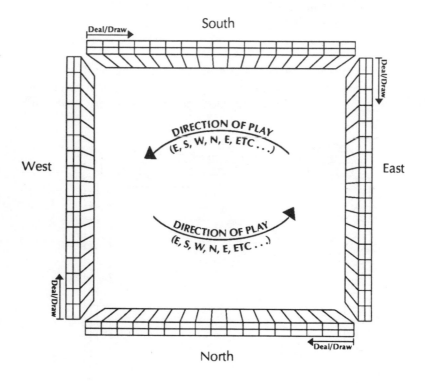

The Deal:

1. a) East (Leader) makes the first draw of 4 Tiles.
Then South, West, and North each draw 4 Tiles.
   b) Each player draws 3 times, 4 Tiles each time for a total of 12 Tiles.

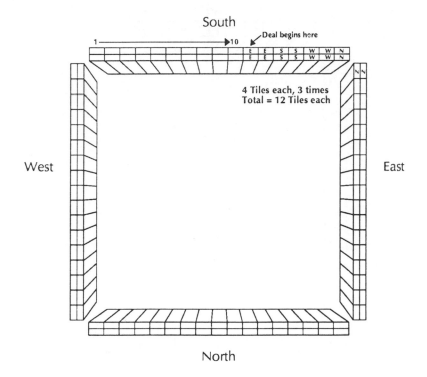

c) East draws 2 Tiles as shown, then South, West and North draw 1 Tile each, as shown.

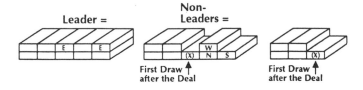

2. The End Wall is marked off. The End Wall always consists of the last 14 Tiles of the Wall. The End Wall is used to signal a Tie Hand, and it is also used as a source of Supplement Tiles (more of these two concepts later).

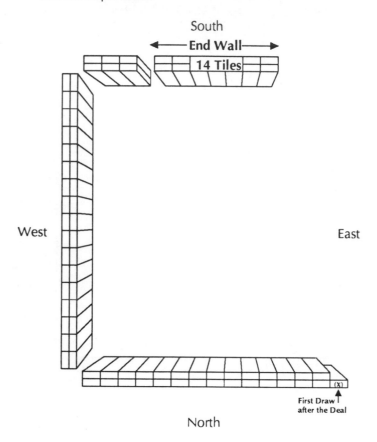

3. East (the Leader) is now holding 14 Tiles, and the other players each hold 13 Tiles.

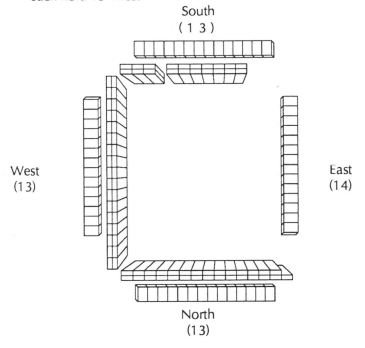

South
(1 3)

West
(13)

East
(14)

North
(13)

The Deal – Summary:

1. The Leader casts 2 dice, counts players in the Directon of Play, **starting with self.**

2. The player designated also casts 2 dice, and totals the numbers of **both** casts.

3. The designated player counts stacks of Tiles, **right to left**, starting on own side of the Wall.

4. Deal begins with **next** 4 Tiles.

5. The Leader (E) takes 4 Tiles, then S, then W, then N, 3 times (Total = 12 Tiles).

6. Last draw for the Deal:

Leader =

Non-Leaders =

First Draw ↑
after the Deal

First Draw ↑
after the Deal

7. Mark off the End Wall (last 14 Tiles).

Beginning the Play:

1. East discards 1 Tile, and does not draw.

Note: The Discards are placed inside the Wall, face up, in a row starting on the player's left.

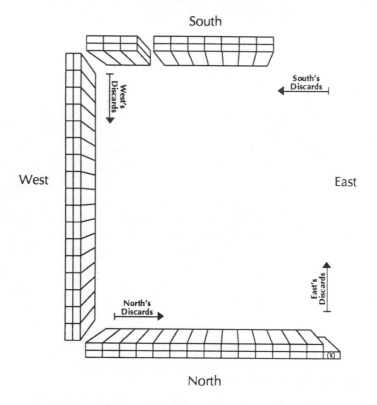

2. Then South draws a Tile and discards, then West, then North, then East (who, from now on draws and discards like the other players).

3. Tiles are drawn from the Wall or, under certain conditions, Discarded Tiles may be claimed instead of drawing from the Wall. The conditions are explained below.

Claiming Discards/Melding Sets:

Only the **last** Discard can be claimed to meld a Set or complete the hand. The Discard can be claimed until just before the next Discard is laid on the table.

To meld a Set, a player,

1. announces that intention,
2. takes the Discard,
3. incorporates it into the Set,
4. lays down the Melded Set visible to the other players, and
5. discards.

A Discard can only be claimed to *complete* a Set or the hand, therefore a player must already possess at least 2 Tiles of a Set or a hand ready to be completed by 1 Tile before a Discard can be claimed.

    1.   A Discard can be claimed to complete a **Run** only if the Tile was discarded by the **preceding player** (or the player on the left). Play continues in the usual manner. No one loses a turn.

    2.   A Discard can be claimed to complete a **Triple** by **any player**. Play continues to the right of the player who just melded the Triple. One or two players may lose a turn.

    3.   A Discard can be claimed to complete a **Quad** by **any player**. The player must already hold a Concealed Triple. Play continues to the right of the player who just melded, and one or two players may lose a turn.

> *Note: The other method to meld a Quad is as follows. The player already holds a Melded Triple and **Self Draws** from the Wall the 4th Tile that completes the Quad. In this case no one loses a turn. A Melded Triple cannot be converted to a Melded Quad with another Discard since a Melded Set can contain only 1 Discard.*
> *—See also, Robbing a Quad, page 19 (#4)*

For each Quad that is formed, the hand must be "supplemented" by 1 Tile to be able to win. More on this next page.

    4.   A Discard can be claimed to **Complete the Hand** by **any player**. In this case only, the Discard may complete the Pair or a Run even though the winner was not next in play after the Discarder. Of course, the Winning Discard may also complete a Triple. *There is no Discard when a player Completes the Hand.*

> *Note: "To Complete the Hand" means to win the hand.*

CONCEALED SETS:

Sets consisting entirely of Self Drawn Tiles are kept concealed in the hand until the player wins.

WHO GETS A DISCARD CLAIMED BY 2 OR 3 PLAYERS:

Whenever a Discard is claimed by more than 1 player, the Discard will be taken by the player with the most powerful purpose for the Discard.

Purpose for the Discard:

Most Powerful ↑ To win
To meld a Triple or a Quad
Least Powerful ↓ To meld a Run

Whenever 2 or 3 players claim the same Discard to win, the Winning Discard will go to the player closest in play to the discarder.

QUADS/SUPPLEMENT TILES:

For each Quad that is formed, the hand must be supplemented by 1 Tile. Whenever a Quad is formed, either Concealed or Melded,

1. that fact is declared,
2. the Quad is displayed,
3. a "Supplement Tile" is drawn from the end of the End Wall, and
4. a Tile is discarded.

A Melded Quad is displayed in the same manner as any other Melded Set. A Concealed Quad is, of course, kept in the hand, but the outer Tiles of the Quad are displayed to the other players.

A Concealed Quad as seen by the player who is holding it

A Quad need not be declared immediately upon the player possessing all 4 of the same Tile (after all, a player has the option to use 3 Tiles in a Triple with the 4th Tile forming part of a Run). However, a Quad can be declared only when it is the player's turn (melding a Quad by adding a Discard to a Concealed Triple is considered the player's turn). Remember that a hand cannot win unless a Supplement Tile is drawn for each Quad. *See also: Claiming Discards/Melding Sets, previous page #3.*

Since the End Wall always contains the last 14 Tiles, Supplement Tiles must be replaced by Tiles from the end of the regular Wall before a Tie is declared. A Tie is explained on the next page.

Winning (Completing the Hand):

The winner will be the first player to complete a hand that contains 1 Pair plus 4 Sets (the Sets can be any combination of Runs, Triples, and/or Quads).

There is no Discard upon winning.

Winning will happen by:

1. Acquiring a Winning **Self Drawn** Tile from the Wall, or
2. Acquiring a Winning **Supplement** Tile from the End Wall, or
3. Claiming a Winning **Discard** from any other player. Even a Run, the Pair (or a Triple) can be completed with the Winning Tile, or
4. **Robbing a Quad**. The Winning Tile is "Robbed" from another player who is melding a Quad by adding a Self Drawn Tile to a Melded Triple. The Quad can be Robbed only at the time that it is being melded.

Upon declaring a Complete Hand, the winner displays the hand to the other players. The hand is Scored, and Payment is made.

Leading, Change of Own Wind, the Round:

If the Leader wins, the Leader keeps Leading.

If a Non-Leader wins, Leading rotates 1 player to the right (counter-clockwise), and all the players assume new Own Winds, with the new Leader assuming East as Own Wind.

Eventually, Leading will have rotated completely around the table (all the players will have been Leader at least once). This is called a "Round". A Round ends just before Leading reverts back to the First Leader.

Tie:

A Tie is declared when no one Completes a Hand by the time that only the 14 Tiles of the End Wall remains. The play stops, and the next player (on the right of the former Leader) becomes new Leader. All the players assume new Own Winds, the Leader being East.

Remember that the End Wall always consists of 14 Tiles, so every Supplement Tile taken from the End Wall (to form Quads), must be replaced by Tiles from the end of the Regular Wall. Please see the Appendix for other possibilities of a Tie.

Complete Game, Round Winds, Double Winds:

A complete game consists of 4 Rounds. A Round consists of the Lead rotating one time around the table. Each Round is designated a "Round Wind". The **first Round** is the **East Round**, the **second** is the **South Round**, next comes the **West Round**, and the game ends at the conclusion of the **4th** or **North Round**. Whenever the Lead reverts back to the First Leader, the Round Wind changes. At that time, the Round Wind marker , shown at the beginning of this book, is changed to indicate the new Round Wind.

A **Double Wind** occurs when the winner's Own Wind matches the Round Wind.

The Leader is the only player who can score a Double Wind in the 1st Round — the Leader is East, the Round Wind is East. In the 2nd Round, only the player with South as Own Wind can score a Double Wind. In the 3rd Round, the player with West Wind can score a Double Wind. And in the 4th and final Round, only the North Wind can score a Double Wind.

Ordinary Wind:

In a Winning Hand, a Wind that is **neither** the winner's **Own Wind nor the Round Wind**, is called an "Ordinary Wind."

Lucky Tiles:

All **3 Dragons**, Green, White, and Red, the winner's **Own Wind** and the **Round Wind** are Lucky Tiles. They can be used for the Pair or for Triples or Quads.

SCORING

A hand is scored in 2 steps:

1. **Points** for winning, the Pair, Sets, Winning Tile, etc... are totaled, and,
2. **Doubles** are applied to the total.

POINTS:

For winning the hand: .... 20 Points

THE PAIR:

Suit Tiles .... 0 pts.
Ordinary Winds (neither Own Wind nor Round Wind) .... 0 pts.
Lucky Pair (any Dragon, Own Wind, or Round Wind) .... 2 pts.
Double Wind (Own Wind matches Round Wind) .... 4 pts.
Note: The terms "Concealed" and "Melded" do not appply to the Pair.

THE SETS:

Runs: .... 0 pts.

Melded Triples:
    Internal Suit Tiles (2's through 8's) .... 2 pts.
    External Suit Tiles (1's or 9's) or Honor Tiles .... 4 pts.

Concealed Triples:
    Internals .... 4 pts.
    Externals or Honors .... 8 pts.

Melded Quads:
    Internals .... 8 pts.
    Externals or Honors .... 16 pts.

Concealed Quads:
    Internals .... 16 pts.
    Externals or Honors .... 32 pts.

Winning Tile (the last Tile to Complete the Hand for the win):
Discarded Tile: ....0 pts.
Tile Self Drawn from the Wall: ....2 pts.
One Chance Tile: ....2 pts.
Occasionally, a hand can be completed by 1 Tile only. This is a **One Chance Tile.**

A One Chance Tile will occur only under the following conditions.

1. The middle Tile of any Run, (X) = One Chance

2. The inside Tile of an "External Run", (X) = One Chance

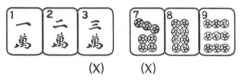

3. Completing the Pair, (X) = One Chance

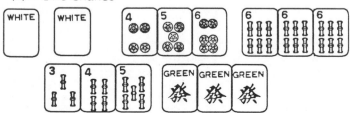

Note: There is one instance in which completing the Pair would not qualify as a One Chance, please see the Appendix.

Concealed Hand except for Discarded Winning Tile ....10 pts.
The entire hand was Self Drawn, except for the Winning Tile, which was a Discard.
A completely concealed winning hand that includes a Self Drawn Winning Tile earns 1 Double.

At this time, all the Points of the winning hand are totaled. Make sure you include all the possibilities for Points, even when there is overlap. For instance, if the Winning Tile is Self Drawn (for 2 pts.) and One Chance (also 2 pts.), 4 Points are added in the Score.

SCORING POINTS – SUMMARY

Winning 20

The Pair:
Suit Tiles 0
Ordinary Winds# 0
Lucky Tiles* 2
Double Wind** 4

Sets:
Runs 0

Melded Triples
Internals...2
Externals or Honors..4

Concealed Triples
Internals...4
Externals or Honors..8

Melded Quads
Internals...8
Externals or Honors..16

Concealed Quads
Internals...16
Externals or Honors..32

Winning Tile:
Discard 0
Self Drawn 2
One Chance 2

Concealed Hand:
Winning Tile a Discard 10
Winning Tile Self Drawn ....1 Double

*Note: #Ordinary Winds are neither Own Wind nor Round Wind.
*Lucky Tiles are all 3 Dragons, Own Wind or Round Wind.
**Double Wind matches Own Wind with Round Wind.*

DOUBLES:

In addition to earning Points, a winning hand may score Doubles. For every Double that is accrued, the total of the Points is multiplied by 2.
0 Doubles = Points
1 Double = (Points) X 2
2 Doubles = (Points) X 2 X 2 = (Points) X 4
3 Doubles = (Points) X 2 X 2 X 2 = (Points) X 8
   etc...

Doubles for Sets:
Each Lucky Triple or Quad ....1 Double
Lucky Tiles include:
   1. All 3 Dragons,
   2. The winner's Own Wind, and
   3. The Round Wind.

Double Wind Triple or Quad ....2 Dbls.
   A Double Wind matches the winner's Own Wind with the Round Wind.

All 4 Sets are Triples and/or Quads,
   with 0, 1, or 2 Sets Concealed ....1 Dbl.
   with 3 Sets Concealed ....2 Dbls.
   with all 4 Sets Concealed .... 500 Points
                         or Limit, see below
   3 Concealed Triples and/or Quads plus 1 Run ....1 Dbl.

Doubles for the Winning Tile:
With a completely Concealed hand ....1 Dbl.
   (Winning Tile Self Drawn. Make sure to include
   2 points for the Self Drawn Winning Tile)
Winning Tile is the last Tile of the Wall ....1 Dbl.
   (The last Tile before the End Wall)
Winning Tile is the last Discard (just before the End Wall)....1 Dbl.
Winning Tile was Robbed from a Quad ....1 Dbl.
   (The Winning Tile was taken from a Quad
   at the time the Quad was melded)
Winning Tile was a Supplement Tile ....1 Dbl.
   (The Winning Tile is drawn from the End Wall
   upon making a Quad)

Doubles for Consistency:

For 3 **consecutive** Runs in the **same Suit** ....1 Dbl.
(1 through 9 of the same Suit in 3 Sets)

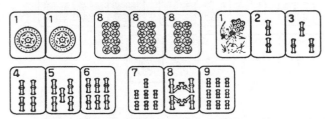

For No Points: ....1 Dbl.

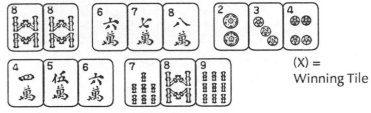

(X) =
Winning Tile

The hand scores only 20 points for the win.
A No Points Hand must meet the following 4 conditions:
1. The Pair consists of Suit Tiles or Ordinary Winds.
2. All 4 Sets are Runs.
3. The Winning Tile was a Discard, and
4. The Winning Tile was not One Chance.

A Concealed Hand with a Discarded Winning Tile (for 10 pts.) can also qualify for a No Points Double. In such case, the total of 30 Points is Doubled.

The Double for No Points, does not exclude the possibility for other Doubles, such as for 3 consecutive Runs in the same suit or many others.

All Internal Suit Tiles: ....1 Dbl.

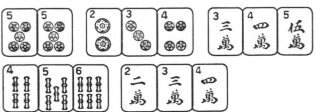

All External Suit Tiles *and* Honor Tiles: ....1 Dbl.

External *or* Honor in each Set: ....1 Dbl.

One Suit *and* Honors: ....1 Dbl.

One Suit Only (includes **Externals and Internals**): ....3 Dbls.

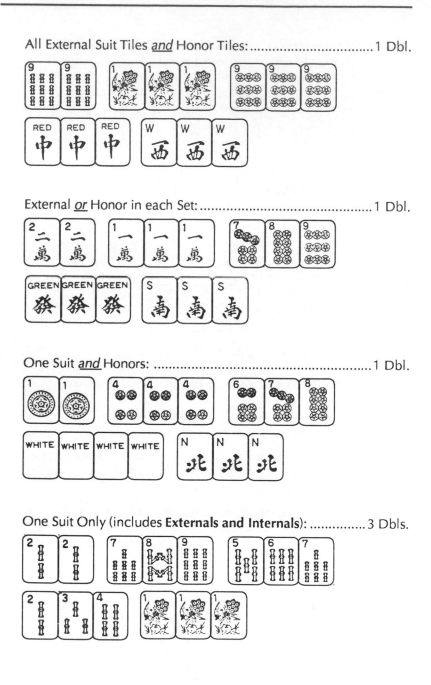

One Suit Only (contains **only Internals**) ....4 Dbls.

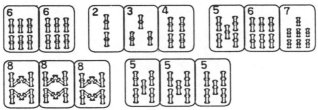

Note: Whitney values the One Suit Only Hand at 4 Doubles, while Kanai and Farrell give it 3 or 4 Doubles as described above.

Little 3 Dragons: ....1 Dbl.
(The Pair and 2 Sets are Dragons)

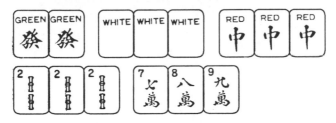

At this time, the Total Score is calculated by Doubling the Points as appropriate.

0 Doubles = Points
1 Double = (Points) X 2

2 Doubles = (Points) X 2 X 2 = (Points) X 4
3 Doubles = (Points) X 2 X 2 X 2 = (Points) X 8

A winning hand may qualify for several types of Doubles simultaneously. In such case, the winning hand is given **all** the Doubles which it earned. For instance, the Winning Hand with a Lucky Set would score 1 Double, and may qualify for a Double with a Suppelment Winning Tile, or a Double for One Suit and Honors, or a Double for a Concealed Winning Hand, etc....

The Total Score is rounded off to the nearest multiple of 10 for the Payment.

SCORING DOUBLES – SUMMARY:

0 Doubles = Points
1 Double = (Points) X 2
2 Doubles = (Points) X 2 X 2 = (Points) X 4
3 Doubles = (Points) X 2 X 2 X 2 = (Points) X 8
 etc . . .

DOUBLES

For Sets:

Each Lucky Set* 1
Double Wind Set** 2

All 4 Sets are Triples and/or Quads:
0, 1, or 2 Sets Concealed 1
3 Sets Concealed 2
4 Sets Concealed ....Limit

3 Concealed Triples or Quads + 1 Run 1

For the Winning Tile:

Concealed Hand (incl. Winning Tile) 1
Last Tile of the Wall 1
Last Discard 1
Robbed from a Quad 1
Supplement Tile 1

For Consistency:

3 consecutive Runs in the same Suit 1
No Points 1
All Internals 1
All Externals <u>and</u> Honors 1
External <u>or</u> Honor in each Set 1
One Suit <u>and</u> Honors 1
One Suit Only (Externals + Internals) 3
One Suit Only (Internals only) 4

Little 3 Dragons (Pair + 2 Sets are Dragons) 1

*Note: * **Lucky Tiles** are all 3 Dragons, Own Wind or Round Wind.*
*****Double Wind** matches Own Wind with Round Wind.*

The Total Score is rounded to the nearest multiple of 10

THE LIMIT (500 POINTS):

No matter what the Total Score adds up to, the maximum value of a Winning Hand cannot exceed 500 points. The Limit is scored after Doubling the Points and before Payment is figured.

The Limit is reached if:
1. The Total Score meets or exceeds the Limit of 500 pts. Or,
2. The Winner completed one of the following Limit Hands.

LIMIT HANDS:

4 Concealed Triples and/or Quads:
(Only the Pair may contain a Discarded Tile).

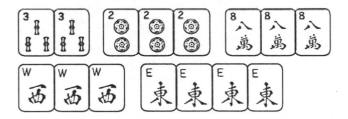

Big 3 Dragons:
3 of the Sets consist of Dragons, the rest of the hand can be any Tiles that will Complete the Hand.

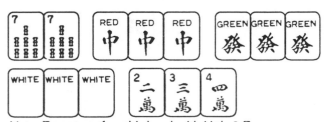

Note: Do not confuse this hand with Little 3 Dragons (valued at 1 Double), see above.

Little 4 Winds:
The Pair and 3 of the Sets consist of the Winds, the 4th Set can be any Set that will Complete the Hand.

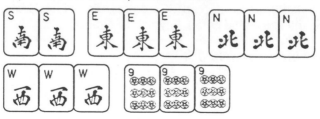

Big 4 Winds:
All 4 Sets consist of the Winds. The Pair can consist of any matching Tiles.

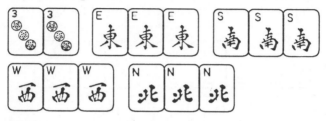

All Honors:
The Pair and all 4 Sets consist only of Honor Tiles.

All Externals:
The Pair and all 4 Sets consist only of External Suit Tiles.

Leader's 1st chance:
The Leader Completes a Hand upon the Deal. Any Complete Hand (1 Pair plus 4 Sets) qualifies for the Limit.

Non-Leader's 1st chance:
A Non-Leader Completes a Hand either,
1. With the **Leader's first Discard,** or,
2. With a **Self Drawn Tile in the first turn**, but before a Set is melded by any player.
Any Complete Hand qualifies for the Limit.

Nine Gates:
A **One Suit Only** Hand consisting of a Triple of 1's, a run from 2 through 8, and a Triple of 9's (total=13 Tiles), plus a Winning Tile that matches any of the others. The 13 Tiles must be all Self Drawn. Only the Winning Tile, also of the same Suit, may be a Discard, but only if it is the matching Tile.

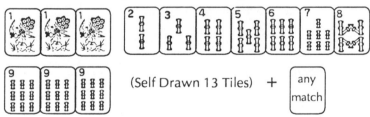

(Self Drawn 13 Tiles) + [any match]

13 Orphans:
1 Tile each of all the External and Honor Tiles (total=13 Tiles), plus a Winning Tile that matches any of the others. Only the Winning Tile may be a Discard, it can be any of the 14 Tiles, it need not be the matching Tile.

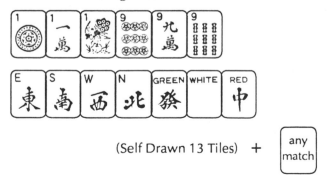

(Self Drawn 13 Tiles) + [any match]

If a player wins 8 hands consecutively **as the Leader**, the 9th and subsequent Winning Hands are automatic Limit Hands (Final Score = 500 Points).

LIMIT HANDS – SUMMARY

LIMIT HANDS (500 Points)

4 Concealed Triples and/or Quads
Big 3 Dragons (3 Sets are Dragons)
Little 4 Winds (Pair + 3 Sets are Winds)
Big 4 Winds (All 4 Sets are Winds)
All Honors
All Externals
Leader's 1st chance
Non-Leaders' 1st chance
Nine Gates (One Suit Only, 1's + 9's + 2 thru 8 + match)
13 Orphans (1 ea. Externals & Honors + match)
Leader's Limit (9th and subsequent wins)

Mah Jong One Step at a Time—Scoring Summary

LIMIT HANDS (500 Points)

4 Concealed Triples and/or Quads
Big 3 Dragons (3 Sets are Dragons)
Little 4 Winds (Pair + 3 Sets are Winds)
Big 4 Winds (All 4 Sets are Winds)
All Honors
All Externals
Leader's 1st chance
Non-Leaders' 1st chance
Nine gates (One suit only: 1's + 9's + 2 thru 8 + match)
13 Orphans (1ea. Externals & Honors + match)
Leader's Limit (9th and subsequent wins, see appendix)

PAYMENT

If the Leader wins Self Drawn:
  Non-Leaders pay Final Score X 2.

If the Leader wins with a Discard:
  The Discarder pays Final Score X 6.

If a Non-Leader wins Self Drawn:
  The Leader pays Final Score X 2, and
  each other Non-Leader pays Final Score.

If a Non-Leader wins with a Discard:
  The Discarder pays Final Score X 4.

Total Score is rounded to nearest 10

San Jose • London

ISHI PRESS INTERNATIONAL

POINTS

Winning 20

The Pair:
Suit Tiles 0
Ordinary Winds# 0
Lucky Tiles* 2
Double Wind** 4

Sets:

Runs		0
Melded Triples	Internals	2
	Externals or Honors	4
Concealed Triples	Internals	4
	Externals or Honors	8
Melded Quads	Internals	8
	Externals or Honors	16
Concealed Quads	Internals	16
	Externals or Honors	32

Winning Tile:
Discard 0
Self Drawn 2
One Chance 2

Concealed Hand:
Winning Tile a Discard 10
Winning Tile Self Drawn ....1 Dbl.

Note: #Ordinary Winds are neither Own Wind nor Round Wind.
*Lucky Tiles are all 3 Dragons, Own Wind or Round Wind.
**Double Wind matches Own Wind with Round Wind.

DOUBLES

For Sets:
Each Lucky Set* 1
Double Wind Set** 2
All 4 Sets are Triples and/or Quads
   0, 1, or 2 Sets Concealed 1
   3 Sets Concealed 2
   All 4 Sets Concealed ....Limit
3 Concealed Triples/Quads + 1 Run 1

Winning Tile: Concealed Hand (incl. Winning Tile) 1
Last Tile of the Wall 1
Last Discard 1
Robbed from a Quad 1
Supplement Tile 1

Consistency: 3 consecutive Runs (in the same Suit) 1
No Points...1
All Internals 1
All Externals and Honors 1
External or Honor in each Set...........1
One Suit and Honors 1
One Suit Only (Externals + Internals)........3
One Suit Only (Internals only) 4

Little 3 Dragons (Pair and 2 Sets are Dragons).............1

Note: *Lucky Tiles are all 3 Dragons, Own Wind or Round Wind.
**Double Wind matches Own Wind with Round Wind.

Summary of the Deal

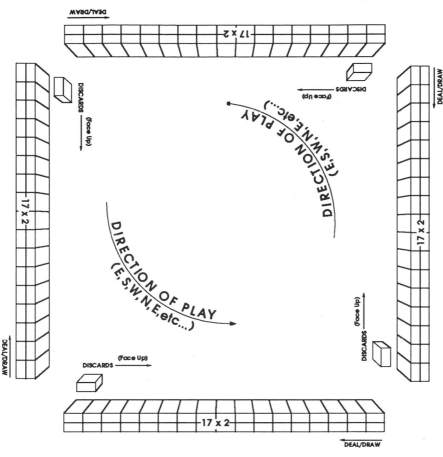

1 - Leader casts 2 dice and counts players in direction of play, starting with self.

2 - Player designated also casts 2 dice and totals numbers of both casts.

3 - Designated player counts tile stacks right to left starting on own side of wall.

4 - Deal begins with the next 4 tiles.

5 - Leader (East) draws the first 4 tiles, then South, then West, then North—3 times for each player. Total=12 tiles.

6 - Last draw for the deal:

Leader:

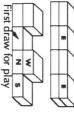

Non-leaders   First draw for play

7 - End Wall=Last 14 tiles.

ISHI PRESS
INTERNATIONAL

PAYMENT

The sticks described at the beginning of this book, or other tokens representing the same denominations, are used to pay the winner.

The amount paid to the winner and who makes the Payment, depend on:

1. **The Final Score:** The Final Score equals the Total Points that are Doubled as appropriate, with the result rounded to the nearest multiple of 10.

2. **Who is the Leader:** The Leader always pays and is always paid double the Final Score.

3. **Whether the Winning Tile was Self Drawn or a Discard:** If the Winning Tile was Self Drawn, all three losers pay the Final Score to the winner, considering double Payment to/from the Leader.

   If the Winning Tile was a Discard, only the Discarder pays the winner. However, the Payment is equal to the total amount the winner would have received from all 3 losers on a Self Drawn Tile. The Leader's double Payment is also considered here.

If the **Leader** wins **Self Drawn** .... Non-Leaders pay Final Score X 2
If the **Leader** wins with a **Discard** .... Discarder pays Final Score X 6

If a **Non-Leader** wins **Self Drawn** .... Leader pays Final Score X 2, and the other Non-Leaders pay Final Score
If a **Non-Leader** wins with a **Discard** ..... Discarder pays Final Score X 4

Note: The Final Score of a Limit Hand (500 points) will still be multipied by the appropriate number for Payment.

SCORING EXERCISES

(C) = Concealed Set   (M) = Melded Set

1. East Round, South player wins on a Self Drawn Winning Tile.

(X) = Winning Tile

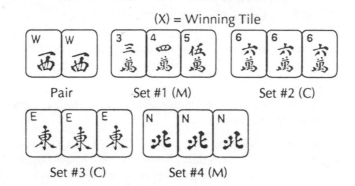

Pair   Set #1 (M)   Set #2 (C)

Set #3 (C)   Set #4 (M)

POINTS
Winning = 20
 Pair = 0
 Set #1 = 0
 Set #2 = 4
 Set #3 = 8
 Set #4 = 4
Winning Tile:
 Self Drawn = 2
 One Chance = 2
Total Points = 40

DOUBLES

Lucky Triple (East is Round Wind) = 1
 One Suit *and* Honors = 1

Total Doubles = 2

Total Score = 40 X 2 X 2 = 160 Points
Final Score (to nearest 10) = 160 Points

PAYMENT:
Leader pays South-160 pts. X 2 = 320 pts.
Non-Leaders pay South-160 pts. each.

Total value of the hand = 320 + 160 + 160 = 640 Points.

2. West Round, West player wins with a Discard from East.

(X) = Winning Tile

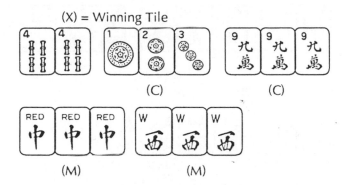

(C)   (C)

(M)   (M)

POINTS
Winning = 20
Pair = 0
Set #1 = 0
Set #2 = 8
Set #3 = 8
Set #4 = 8

DOUBLES
Lucky Triple (Red Dragon) = 1
Double Wind Triple (West Wind) = 2
External or Honor in each Set = 1

Total Doubles = 4

Winning Tile:
One Chance = 2
Total Points = 46

Total Score = 46 X 2 X 2 X 2 X 2 = 766 Points
Final Score = Limit, 500 points

PAYMENT
Leader pays West 500 pts. X 4 = 2000 pts.
Total value of the hand = 2000 pts.

3. South Round, East wins with a Discard from West.

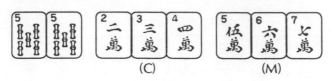

(C)   (M)

(X) = Winning Tile

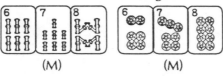

(M)   (M)

POINTS
Winning = 20
Pair = 0
All Sets = 0
Winning Tile = 0

Total Points = 20

DOUBLES
No Points = 1
All Internals = 1

Total Doubles = 2

Total Score = 20 X 2 X 2 = 80 pts.
Final Score = 80 pts.

PAYMENT
West pays East = 80 X 6 = 480 pts.
Total value of the hand = 480 pts.

THE DEAL– SUMMARY

(Ex. : East rolls 6, South is designated and rolls 4, Total = 10)

1. a) East (Leader) makes the first draw of 4 Tiles.
        Then South, West, and North each draw 4 Tiles.
    b) Each player draws 3 times, 4 Tiles each time for a total
        of 12 Tiles.

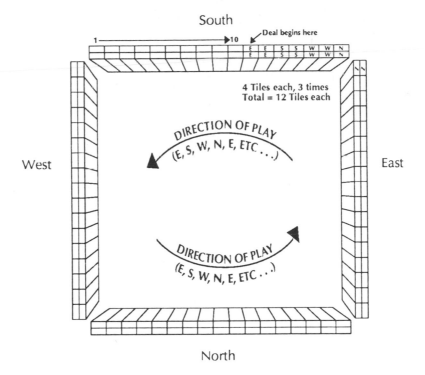

c) East draws 2 Tiles as shown, then South, West and North
    draw 1 Tile each, as shown.

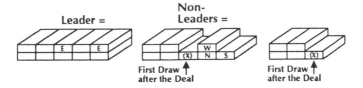

2. The End Wall is marked off. The End Wall always consists of the last 14 Tiles of the Wall. The End Wall is used to signal a Tie Hand, and it is also used as a source of Supplement Tiles .

South

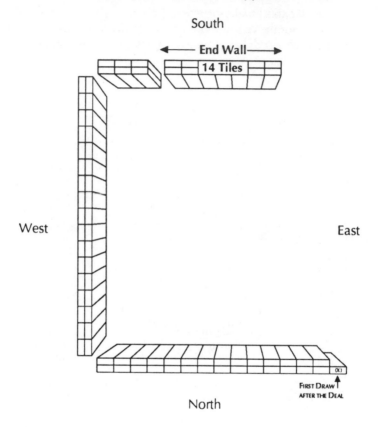

West

East

North

First Draw
After the Deal

3. East (the Leader) is now holding 14 Tiles, and the other players each hold 13 Tiles.

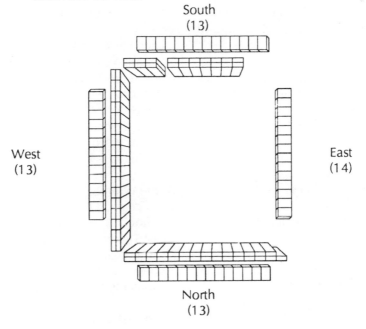

South
(13)

West
(13)

East
(14)

North
(13)

THE DEAL – SUMMARY:

1. The Leader casts 2 dice, counts players in the Directon of Play, **starting with self.**
2. The player designated also casts 2 dice, and totals the numbers of **both** casts.
3. The designated player counts stacks of Tiles, **right to left**, starting on own side of the Wall.
4. Deal begins with **next** 4 Tiles.
5. The Leader (E) takes 4 Tiles, then S, then W, then N, 3 times (Total = 12 Tiles).
6. Last draw for the Deal:

7. Mark off the End Wall (last 14 Tiles).

SCORING SUMMARY

POINTS

Winning 20

The Pair:
Suit Tiles 0
Ordinary Winds# 0
Lucky Tiles* 2
Double Wind** 4

Sets:
Runs 0
Melded Triples
Internals 2
Externals or Honors 4
Concealed Triples
Internals 4
Externals or Honors 8
Melded Quads
Internals 8
Externals or Honors 16
Concealed Quads
Internals 16
Externals or Honors 32

Winning Tile:
Discard 0
Self Drawn 2
One Chance 2
Concealed Hand:
Winning Tile a Discard 10
Winning Tile
Self Drawn .... 1 Dbl.

DOUBLES

For Sets:
Each Lucky Set* 1
Double Wind Set** 2
All 4 Sets are Triples and/or Quads
0, 1, or 2 Sets Concealed 1
3 Sets Concealed 2
4 Sets Concealed .... Limit
3 Concealed Triples or
Quads + 1 Run 1

For the Winning Tile:
Concealed Hand
(incl. Winning Tile) 1
Last Tile of the Wall 1
Last Discard 1
Robbed from a Quad 1
Supplement Tile 1

For Consistency:
3 consecutive Runs in the
same Suit 1
No Points 1
All Internals 1
All Externals *and* Honors 1
External *or* Honor in
each Set 1
One Suit *and* Honors 1
One Suit Only (Externals +
Internals) 3
One Suit Only (Internals only) 4
Little 3 Dragons 1
(Pair and 2 Sets are Dragons)

Note: **#Ordinary Winds** are neither Own Wind nor Round Wind.
Lucky Tiles are all 3 Dragons, Own Wind or Round Wind.
****Double Wind** matches Own Wind with Round Wind.

(Total Score is rounded to nearest 10)

LIMIT SUMMARY

- 4 Concealed Triples and/or Quads
- Big 3 Dragons (3 Sets are Dragons)
- Little 4 Winds (Pair + 3 Sets are Winds)
- Big 4 Winds (All 4 Sets are Winds)
- All Honors
- All Externals
- Leader's 1st chance
- Non-Leaders' 1st chance
- Nine gates (One Suit Only, 1's + 9's + 2 thru 8 + match)
- 13 Orphans (1ea. Externals & Honors + match)
- Leader's Limit (9th and subsequent wins)

PAYMENT SUMMARY

If the **Leader** wins **Self Drawn**:
> Non-Leaders pay Final Score X 2.

If the **Leader** wins with a **Discard**:
> The Discarder pays Final Score X 6.

If a **Non-Leader** wins **Self Drawn**:
> The Leader pays Final Score X 2, and
> each other Non-Leader pays Final Score.

If a **Non-Leader** wins with a **Discard**:
> The Discarder pays Final Score X 4.

APPENDIX

The purpose of this section is to introduce new concepts and to discuss rules for situations that occur infrequently. I suggest that you become thoroughly familiar with the main body of this manual before you study this appendix. The information that follows is not crucial to the enjoyment of Mah Jong for the beginner.

OFFICIAL TERMINOLOGY:

Throughout this manual, I have introduced my own terminology. Therefore when you play with someone for the first time, you may need to define certain terms. You will find, however, that the ideas and the concepts are basically the same. Please remember that there are several versions of this game throughout the world. Still, the variations can be understood with a little observation and a few questions.

CLAIMING DISCARDS:

Officially, "Chow!" or "Chi!" is exclaimed when a player intends to claim a Discard to meld a Run, "Pung!" to meld a Triple, "Kong!" to meld a Quad or to declare a Concealed Quad, "Out!" or "Lon!" to declare a Winning Hand. I find these terms superfluous, and at times intimidating to the novice, so I do not encourage their use. However, using these terms may speed playing for the experienced player, and since many people use them, I present them here.

THE COMPLETE HAND:

Since there is no Discard upon winning, a Complete Hand will contain between 14 and 18 Tiles, depending on the number of Quads. With each Quad, the hand increases by 1 (Supplement) Tile.

ROBBING A QUAD:

Though I have not found the official rule for this situation, I think the Winning Tile Robbed from a Quad should be considered a Discard for the purposes of Scoring and Payment. And, of course, the player whose Quad was Robbed is liable for the entire Payment.

MELDING SETS:

Officially, when melding a Run, the Discard is laid sideways. When melding a Triple or a Quad, a Tile is also laid sideways, but in this case it indicates which player discarded the Tile that completed the Set. The Tile(s) in the *center* of the Melded Triple or Quad indicate(s) that the Tile was discarded by the player sitting *opposite* the melding player. The Tile on the *right* of the Melded Triple or Quad indicates that the discarder is sitting on the *right* of the melding player. And, of course, the Tile on the *left* indicates that the discarder is sitting on the *left* .

Note: Since the Discard in a Melded Run always comes from the preceding player (on the left), we only need to indicate which Tile in the Run is the Discard.

This procedure is of great interest to the experienced player who wants to keep track of which player discarded which Tile.

Also, when comes the time to Score, it is easy to distinguish the Concealed from the Melded Sets by following these procedures.

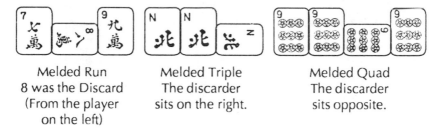

Melded Run	Melded Triple	Melded Quad
8 was the Discard	The discarder	The discarder
(From the player	sits on the right.	sits opposite.
on the left)		

WINNING TILE:

For an easy way to keep track of the Winning Tile, place it on top of the Set it completes. If it is Self Drawn, turn it "up and down" just like the other Tiles. If it is a Discard, turn it sideways.

WINNING TILE MATCHES A PREVIOUS DISCARD (CALLED *"SAFE DISCARD"*):

A player, say "X" may not claim a Discard from, say "Y" **for the win** if "X" has previously discarded the same Tile, unless "X" has drawn from the Wall since discarding the Tile in question.

ONE CHANCE TILE:

There are 2 types of hands whereby the Winning Tile completes the Pair. Only 1 of these hands is considered One Chance, the hand illustrated in the Scoring Section — the 4 Sets are complete, plus 1 Tile independent of all the others.

The other type of hand whereby the Winning Tile completes the Pair is not One Chance because it can be completed with either of 2 Tiles. This hand contains 3 complete Sets with the 4th Set being a 4 Tile run. Such a hand can be completed by matching either of the 2 outside Tiles of the run, for the Pair.

(X) = Discarded Winning Tile

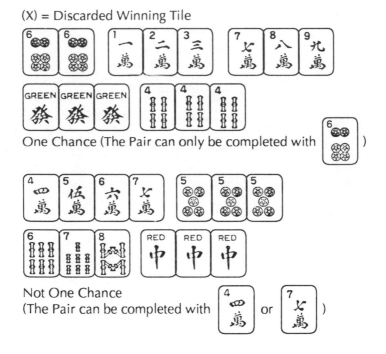

One Chance (The Pair can only be completed with [6 dots])

Not One Chance
(The Pair can be completed with [4 萬] or [7 萬])

Other Ties:

In addition to the Tie described in the main text (reaching the 14 Tiles of the End Wall), there are other ways to arrive at a Tie. Remember that the End Wall must contain 14 Tiles. Any Supplement Tile drawn from the End Wall must be replaced by Tiles from the end of the Regular Wall. In this case, new hands are dealt. Leading rotates 1 player to the right.. All the players assume new Own Winds, with the new Leader being East.

If more than 1 player makes 4 Quads in the same hand, the game stops, new hands are dealt, and all the players keep their Own Wind. The Leader does not change.

A Tie will occur when all 4 players discard the same Wind during the **1st round of discarding** at the beginning of playing a hand. New hands are dealt. Leading rotates 1 player to the right, and all the players assume new Own Winds (of course, the Leader is East).

Penalties:

Officially, penalties are imposed for a variety of errors in declarations or to claim a Discard. I prefer to play without the onus of a penalty. In a friendly game where only points are at stake, penalties may detract from having fun. If your game offers higher stakes, you will need to agree on a system of penalties before playing.

I suggest the following consequences for breaking some rules:

If a player makes a wrong declaration or claim for a Discard, allow the player to "take it back" and forgive.

If a player happens to be missing Tiles in the hand, the player ends with the hand still short, and cannot win that hand.

If a player holds too many Tiles, the player finishes the hand with extra Tiles, and is not allowed to win that hand.

OPTIONAL RULES:

As I stated in the Introduction, there are variations on the game of Mah Jong. The rules discussed until now are based on the official version developed by the Japan Mah Jong Association. I suggest you discuss which set of rules you will follow before you start a game with new people.

Following are some optional unofficial rules you may wish to adopt:

OPTIONAL NO POINTS DOUBLE:

A player may be given 1 Double for a No Points Hand when the Winning Tile was Self Drawn and/or One Chance, if the winner foregoes the 2 Points each for Self Drawn and/or One Chance Tile. The same hand should still be given any other Doubles for which it qualifies, such as Concealed Hand with Self Drawn Tile (1 Dbl.), or 3 consecutive Runs in the same Suit (1 Dbl.), etc...

OPTIONAL DOUBLE FOR A READY HAND:

A hand that needs only 1 Tile to be complete is said to be "Ready". A Ready Hand need not be One Chance. A player declares Ready, only during his or her turn, by placing a 100-point token in the center of the Wall and turning sideways the Tile discarded at that time. The 100 Points will go to the winner of that hand.

A **declared** Ready Hand earns 1 Double.

A Ready Hand must meet **all** the following criteria to qualify for the Double:

1. The Ready Hand must be **completely concealed**, it may include a Concealed Quad.
2. **No changes** are permitted after the hand is declared Ready. No Quads may be made, even if Concealed.
3. The Ready Hand must incorporate **the very next Tile** that will complete it , even if it is not the most preferred Tile, or even if it is a Discard.
4 The declaration **cannot be cancelled.**
5. You may be required to **lay down your hand, face down**. You may be prevented to look at any part of your hand again until someone wins.

The Complete Hand is composed of 7 Pairs. By its nature, this hand is Concealed when Ready, only the Winning Tile may be a Discard. None of the Pairs are repeated (in other words, it contains no Quad).

The 7 Pairs Hand automatically earns 100 Points.

The 7 Pairs Hand may also qualify for many Doubles, such as 1 Double each for a Ready Hand (if adopted), for All Internals, for the Last Tile of the Wall, and others.

Books from Ishi Press

Books about Go
G30: An Introduction to Go
G41: The Magic of Go
G31: The Second Book of Go
G2: Basic Techniques of Go
G28: Lessons in the Fundamentals of Go
G10: In the Beginning
G11: 38 Basic Joseki
G12: Tesuji
G13: Life and Death
G14: Attack and Defense
G15: The Endgame
G16: Handicap Go
G6: Strategic Concepts of Go
G18: Test Your Go Strength
G19: Breakthrough to Shodan
G27: Kato's Attack and Kill
G32: The Power of the Star Point
G34: All About Thickness
G44: The 3-3 Point
G45: Positional Judgment
G21, G22, G23: Dictionary of Basic Joseki (3 vols)
Invincible: The Games of Shusaku
Go and the World of Japanese Prints
G40: The World of Go

Other Oriental Strategy Games
S1: Shogi for Beginners
S4: Chinese Chess for Beginners
S5: Mah Jong One Step at a Time
SH51: The Game of Mah Jong Illustrated
SH52: Improve Your Mah Jong

Go World Magazine
Go World is a regular quarterly magazine that provides comprehensive coverage of professional Go combined with instructional and background articles on the game. Must reading for all serious players.　FOL

APR 1 7 2024